THE LIGHT, THE HEAVY, AND THE DARK

I don't think I'll ever be exceptional at anything if I'm not exceptionally honest about my failures and shortcomings.

—Gary Robert Childress

THE LIGHT, THE HEAVY, AND THE DARK

The Collected Poetry of
Gary Robert Childress

Edited by Elaine Person

Published by CHB Media

ISBN: 9798393560584

Library of Congress Control Number: 2023938212

First Edition
Printed in the USA

DEDICATION

This book is dedicated to the memory of my late father, Robert Eli Childress III, to Catherine H. who is always in my thoughts and hopes, and to her daughter, Ashley, who is always in her mom's thoughts and hopes.

ACKNOWLEDGMENTS

I'd like to thank my parents, Katherine and Robert who kept me alive during my darkest, most crippling episodes of paranoia, fear, and despair. Without their unwavering love and care, I would not, in all likelihood, be here today. Thank you to The National Alliance on Mental Illness for their support and advocacy. And special thanks to poet and writing instructor Elaine Person for working with me to get this book edited and published. Without her generous efforts, there would be no pages following this one.

THE POEMS

Chapter One: Light Fare

Chapter Three: Dark Thoughts

Chapter One
Light Fare

Abilify

I don't know why
Abilify
works on me as well as it does
However, it's been
good medicine
that keeps me stable while on the drug

Haldol, a curse
was so much worse
I never want to be on it again
although it may have calmed me
it turned me into a zombie
and that's the worst I've ever been

Acrimony on Sesame Street

It was a day full of acrimony
for Bert and Ernie
and Oscar
as they tried to discuss good hygiene

"What on earth do you mean?"
Oscar exclaimed

"You can't be serious,"
Ernie's reply came

Ernie felt frustrated
in trying to explain
so he turned to Bert
and said,
"I don't know what to tell him
for whatever it's worth."

After some hesitation
Bert studied the situation
and came upon a strategy with resolve
"We'll tell him it means *dirtiness*
and our problem will be solved!"

Apathy

Apathy...can often be
a very terrible disease
It's something some
can't overcome
including me

Sometimes I wish
to simply sit
and stare off into space

And other times
I'm just as fine
to lie in bed most of the day

It doesn't matter
if I'd rather
do one thing or the other

because neither one
gets anything done
and really isn't worth the bother

Being Fifty-two

I'm fifty-two
maybe a late bloomer
I wish I'd matured
a little sooner

But now is fine
as I approach the close
of life

Still...
sooner would have been nice

Bipolar with Psychotic Features

I've had many diagnoses
since I first fell ill in 1991
the latest one
from a psychologist
is bipolar with psychotic features

However, the DSM*
has always been
very vague and imprecise
and apparently I've been misdiagnosed once or twice
so I'm skeptical
and cynical
and not sure I believe her

*Diagnostic and Statistical Manual of Mental Disorders (DSM-5-TR)

Blessed

Having all I need
but not everything I want
is the greatest gift

Broken

I had a brain but it broke
Now I take pills
because I'm quite ill
They don't completely fix it, though

Candace

I still think of Candace sometimes
She was *cool*
beyond any possible comparison
popular and nice
She was a love of my life
and I was a fool
not to seek out to marry her

But I was young
and very immature
and I'm sure
everything happened for the best

And even if it didn't
life really isn't
all that bad

So for that reason
I still feel
Very blessed

Entitlement

A psychologist I once visited
concluded that I may have
feelings of entitlement

I'm not entirely sure what she meant
and when I asked for clarification
she didn't give a clear explanation
But I assume it's some kind of deficiency
possessed by me
which I need to fix
for my own recuperation

Getting Back on Meds

I went off my meds
for a while last year
I never want to go off them again
I've been on and off them many times before
However, it has become clear
from repeated trial and error
that life without meds
is something I cannot afford

They prevent delusions
and help control periodic depression
and although they may bring apathy
my parents would certainly agree with me
without question
that I'm much better on the meds
than without
So now I take them somewhat religiously
with very few exceptions

Hacku: Recipe for Toast

Toaster and sliced bread
Insert bread and press lever
Butter if needed

Hallmark Poem #1

May you live in peace
and recover in good health
surrounding yourself
with loved ones
and people who care
people who will be there
when things are going well
and when they are not
even if life
didn't turn out
quite the way you thought
or hoped

So hang on tight
for the sake of life
it can still mean a lot
to have a good friend
who'll write a goofy poem
just for you
The end

I should work for Hallmark

Hallmark Poem #2

In the end
there's nothing more important
than having a good friend
someone to whom
you can send
a silly poem

Iamb Not Poetic

In misty hills of north Virginia
The honeysuckle thickets growing
By mountain springs so clear delightful
Echoing sounds of town musicians
Who sing ballads of lore and legend
Do take me back to days of childhood
In times of safety free of danger
We swam and fished in flowing rivers
Collected wealth of spring's abundance

The days of youth retreat before us
Memories fade but are not forgotten
As population grows immensely
Now spend my time as thoughts do linger
In misty hills of north Virginia

Improving

I've always had a roof over my head
food to eat
and a bed
in which to sleep

Many in this world
are not so fortunate
and I've not seen anything yet
of how bad things can get

So I'm thankful`
and grateful
though I wish I were wiser
and more knowledgeable

But at least knowing
how foolish I'm being
is a good step on the way
to further growing
and slowly improving
for a better future

Insomnia

I'm feeling tired
and uninspired
but unable to go to sleep
Too much caffeine
does that to me

So in the meantime
I'll compile a rhyme
or two
or three

Meds

I don't like taking meds
They cause weight gain
tremors and apathy
I'd much rather be
off of them instead

But then I'd be insane
depressed, unhappy
and lying all day in bed

I miss the times
when I cared deeply about things
while feeling intensely alive

It's just not the same
Taking these chemicals
That dull and fog my mind

However, it's far, far worse
to have hallucinations, delusions,
and severe depression,
so at the doctor's suggestion,
I've come to the conclusion
to stay on these pills
and follow his directions

Moderation

I like wine
but not all the time
I'll do a little liquor too
But I drink responsibly
and in moderation
It seems like the right thing to do

A little red zin
now and then
A Captain and Coke
but not too many
I once tried a dirty martini

But it really didn't appeal to me
so I tried something else
Now I drink Kahlúa and cream
It tastes like chocolate milk

and you can't go wrong
with chocolate milk

No Hurry, No Worry

I'd rather be happy
Than be a great success
I know it's just not *American*
Not to be the very best
But what was killing me
was not the failure to succeed
but rather all the stress
and worry
of thinking I had to make it
in a hurry
and outpace all the rest

Ode to Antipsychotics

I dedicate this ode
to all of those
who, like me,
have to be
on anti-psychotics

For without them
or similar medicines
things would be much more chaotic

They give us much assistance
Thank God for their existence
Their effects are quite dramatic
To keep us from being manic

Before their very arrival
The struggle for survival
Was no doubt much more brutal
And probably often futile

So let us applaud
Just because
We're thankful for being alive

And though life is not easy
I hope you'll agree with me
The alternative is far worse

Ode to Catherine

I would like to take a moment
to commend
a good friend
named Catherine

She taught me to be thankful
for what I have
for I have a great deal more
than many others do

She taught me what it is
to once again truly live
and to change for the better
in ways that really matter

So thank you

Thank you
for all you have done for me
and all you continue to do
You've made me want to live again
and love again
and that means a lot to me
my platonic friend
And I will try my best
to always be true

Ode to Prozac

Prozac is a happy drug
I take it almost every evening
Though from time to time I may forget
It seems to give my life some meaning

I'd be quite ill
Without the pills
And maybe even suicidal
And though I often lack expression
It keeps me free from much depression
And so I judge it rather vital

Pecked On

Growing up I had many nervous habits
Perhaps they were more of a *disorder*

It hurt my status
For many years
Among my peers
And put me at the bottom
of the pecking order

But despite feeling profoundly sad
From all the pecking that I had had
To deal with
I myself acted just as bad
Toward others I encountered

So being just the same
I don't hold others to blame
Or feel resentful
For all the hurt
That I felt

Rather as I see it
Justice was served
I got what I deserved
But it's over
And these days I'm doing well

Persevering

I can dance
I can sing
And rhyme
And sometimes
I feel on top of the world

Other times I'm lonely and depressed
But I guess
It just might
Be a part of life

The ups and downs
Come and go
And I know
There will be more of both

For tomorrow
There will doubtless be
More joy and sorrow
Ahead for me

However
While I'm here
I must persevere
And never
Ever
Give up before the end

Because
Life may be a journey
Or it may be a race
And even though sometimes
The bad is more than I want to face

The good comes back too
And makes it all worth while
To smile
And stick around
For a little longer
In this place

Philosophy

Philosophy
Was once very dear to me
However, now I have trouble
And struggle
Keeping up with it

There's so much confusion
And very few solutions
To the problems
And concerns
Which many have yearned
For centuries
To solve

I'd rather be happy
And so I play games
And other things
Which are pleasing
To me

I guess I'm a hedonist
And that's the reason which
Causes me to feel terribly embarrassed
And wrong

But some of the time
I'm perfectly fine
And could care less about it
While I play on and on

After Submitting to Haikuniverse

With chances slim
to none, I hit *Submit*
then count the hours
until I see her again—
a fool in love

Politics

I know it's difficult
Not to get political

But I've had too many arguments
and lost too many friends
It's just not worth it in the end

I feel it's just as well
to avoid the fuss
than to discuss
things that divide us
...so I don't talk about it
quite as much
as I did before

However, sometimes
it seems almost impossible
to look the other way
from those responsible
for so much misery and suffering
that happens in our world today

However,
all of us are human
and I'd rather have peace
than have a revolution
where even more may be seriously hurt

And for what it's worth
being idealistic
can make a person seriously pessimistic
So I'm a bit cynical
when it comes to discussing the political
and abstain from it as best I can

Quatern without Refrain

If I had to describe my moods
In a manner most judicious
All the ways I rejoice or brood
I would use the word capricious

If I seem unstrung or serene
Somehow attentive or distant
Or act in manners unforeseen
You may call me inconsistent

No need for worry, stress, nor fear
Be it the case I change at will
You may just think me insincere
You may call me mentally ill

But whether in this matter
I'm ill or temperamental
I say I would choose the latter
Than a label detrimental

Religion

It may be a bit odd
but I don't know if there is a God
so I call myself agnostic

It's a difficult decision
whether or not to practice religion
or else be an atheist

Some may say I'll go to hell
though it's kind of hard
For me to tell
because if anyone can
God should understand
so I'm not worried about it
all that much

Romance

Romantic love is a wonderful thing
I wish I'd experienced it more in life
It would have been nice

But I was immature
awkward
and now wish
I hadn't made such a fool
of myself

I thought the world
of many pretty girls
and now think of missed
opportunities

But back then love was so new to me
that I didn't know what I was doing
fumbling around in the dark
at the very start
of my dating life

Now I'm single
and sometimes wish I had a wife

But I'm beginning to appreciate
more than ever before
that I'm free
to do what I please
and have quite a bit of fun
even without romantic love

Satisfactory Complaint

Things could be worse
or they could be better
But whenever
I think about it,
I think first
of what could be worse

If things were better
I could not complain
So then again
I'd not be happy
just the same

For if I could not complain
then that of which
I could not do
would just as soon
bother me too

Therefore
if I am asked
how am I?
it seems to me
I ought to reply
that things are worse
though I am fine.

Sleep Apnea

I have sleep apnea
It leaves me drowsy
long after I awake
and makes
me forgetful

It's not that great
Being tired all day long
and low on energy
So I tried several times
to use a CPAP machine

However, it didn't help
because I have always felt
awkward wearing a mask
in bed
So I gave it up at last
and sleep now
without one instead

I don't like tempting fate
She can sometimes be unforgiving
But, knock on wood
(because I should)
as of writing this
I'm still living.

Still Caring

After many psychoses
and several diagnoses
I think it safe to say
that my mind
is not at all too well

I've had ups and downs
Seen, thought, and heard
many crazy things
But now
I'm stabilized,
on meds
and realize
it's not the worst
that it can get

And although
I may be a little
despondent and despairing
I haven't completely quit caring
or given up
at least not yet

Poem for Sarah

Living with a mental illness
Is not so bad
I'm still glad
To be alive

I've had some strange delusions
Most of them paranoid and quite bizarre
But so far
So good
And knock on wood
I've survived

The Eternal Return

Recurring nightmare
Running late for an exam
But I'm not in school

The Forgone Wife:
Quatern mostly in Iambic Tetrameter

I dedicate this poem to
a lovely girl that I once knew
Her name was Laurie, fair and bright
I thought of her both day and night

Laurie, so fond I grew of you
I dedicate this poem to
I'd like to hug and hold you close
For you're the one I think of most

A wondrous life I could have had
with you. I think I'd be a dad
I dedicate this poem to
Laurie, the one who makes me blue

For now I wish I'd asked her out
instead of being shy with doubt
But then Laurie would not be who
I dedicate this poem to

The Woken Class

Long, long ago
Father, Son, and Holy Ghost
proclaimed a kingdom
for the least who waited most

The least who waited most
up until then had finished last
which caused much disapproval
from some in the past

So some in the present
came together for now
and came up with a plan
to help the least do better somehow

And for a while things worked well
as the least waited less
until a few thought maybe
the least were doing better than the rest

Arguments got bitter
and controversy grew
as some tried to determine
who should do better than who

Some thought most
to think first of the least
and cautioned others
against historical repeats

Others thought perhaps
it should be based on merit
still others thought maybe
everyone should equally share it

And even on all those things
all could not agree
concerning whether or not
humans should even intervene

However, I suppose
to put a bright spin on the matter
concern for the least at least
got us all talking together

And whether or not
this be sensible or perverse
if everyone agreed
things might just be worse

Together (With COVID)

What is there not to be depressed about?
especially when you're this stressed out
over viruses and economies
and what may happen to you and me
and loved ones
and fellow humans
when all of this is done

What is going on?
Why is this happening?
Will we all make it through?

I don't know whether to cross my fingers
or pray
or if it's all in vain
but I'll still try
just the same
because it seems like all we can do

And this could only be the beginning
Maybe we haven't yet seen anything
of how bad it can be
the territory
we're getting into

But we try not to lose our humanity
to instead face all the uncertainty
and danger
with strength
and compassion
not with fear, anger,
or inaction

and hopefully
with optimism
we'll make it through this cataclysm...

together

The Offer

I accepted a job offer Friday
I'm excited but nervous
and afraid of getting in
over my head
so I'm not breathing a sigh of relief
just yet

Instead
between breaths
I pray to succeed
in doing my job well
because I'll be working
regularly
with the mentally ill
and they mean a lot to me

Because deep down inside
having such an illness myself
I have always felt
that they are my tribe
and I really want to help
them live better lives

Unbecoming of Age

I don't think I've yet come of age
In some ways it's a shame
and in other ways I feel just fine
but my feelings change
from time to time

At age fifty-three
I still live with my folks
but I've lived a good life
though I've never had children
nor taken a wife
as have most

And if I perish
before due time comes
I'll still cherish
the life I've had
because it's been much better
than that of some

Wellbutrin

Wellbutrin
an anti-depressant
helps keep my mood enjoyable
and pleasant

And stable

I take it around seven
or when I get out of bed
every morning
thus ensuring
a better day ahead

Oh Wretched Fortune Cookie

"You will soon be crossing great waters"

Oh great waters
how great thou are
so great and vast
that alas
I cannot count
with both fingers
and toes combined
the sum total
of thy greatness

Thou art greater
than the greatest lake
of Superior
greatest of the great lakes
but possessing
of less greatness
than thou

How I try to contemplate
thy greatness of dimension
yet fail

Thy extension
is far greater than any other
and thy depth far deeper

So great are thou
that I dare not cross thee
for fear
thou may
become cross with me
in return

Yet cross thee
I shall
regardless
sayeth oh
most wretched
of fortune cookies

So wicked
and full of avarice
am I
forsake me not
oh great waters
for thy wrath
is eternal hell
and thy favor
the greatest reward

I desire
the crossing of thee
with the greatest anticipation
though the greatness
of my anticipation
compares not
To thy own greatness

Chapter Two
Heavy Topics

The Safe Harbor

An early morning interlude
sitting in quiet solitude
on a rickety and rusty old dock
while out to sea I longingly watch
gulls soaring gracefully by
in a glorious crimson and amber sky
stretching above placid and gentle waves
for it appears the sea is calm today

I think of countless times before
when I had wandered this lonely shore
in search of another for companionship
someone special to share life with
and when the fateful day finally came
when I had found someone else much the same
we quietly passed each other by
perhaps we'll never know just why

Afterwards I casually soak in the view
then leave for home when the day is through
hoping others who are solitary too
may enjoy their turn
on that rickety and rusty old dock

A Trilogy of Triolets

Down the Triolet: Ominous Warnings

Throughout our lives the seasons changed
But ice is melting everywhere
Now things will never be the same
Throughout our lives the seasons changed
The ecosystems are in strain
When will our leaders ever care?
Throughout our lives the seasons changed
But ice is melting everywhere!

Triolet Backup: The Malicious Mutation

In order to make history
we ought to preserve the future
In fact we create misery
in order to make history
It must be some psychopathy
Deep down we are abusers
In order to make history
we ought to preserve the future

Stopping the Triolets: My Epitaph

It must be nice to be famous
Perhaps it could happen to me
Hubris, can you really blame us?
It must be nice to be famous
Instead it seems it's shame on us
For wanting notoriety
It must be nice to be famous
Perhaps it could happen to me

Anticlimactic

Such is life
like mayflies in spring
late bloomers flap our trepid wings

Throughout summer and autumn
we bided our time

Now winter has finally come
and when the frost has left
we shall all be gone
one by one

Complaining

I don't like to complain
and so I try to abstain
from it

But then again maybe I do
because I'm always trying to
no matter how much I'm cognizant
of it

However,
many have it worse
and I must think of them too
so I bite my tongue and pretend
that it's wrong to complain
when I do

Decay

Fleeting bloom
Thinking of you every day
Time not on your side

Delusions of Grandeur

Excessive ambition
has brought me profound feelings
of futility and inadequacy

The desire for glory
that I could never achieve
has caused me too much frustration
from unrealistic aspirations

And although I still hold them dear
it's becoming painfully clear
at the age of fifty-two
that their realization
was only ever fantasy
and make-believe

And in the end
I'll lose them too

Depression

Depression is
an obsession of mine
I seem to have it
so much of the time

It comes and goes
ebbs and flows
and then subsides

It's a kind of gravity I feel inside

It's when I walk
in solitude and loneliness
in a crowded public place

It's when I feel defeated
and want to bury my head in bed
to hide my face

It's when a pretty girl walks by
and doesn't say "hello" when I say "hi"

It's when I feel empty and hollow
like merely a shell
but that's just life
when things aren't going very well

Dissociates

I see you staring out there again
I wonder what it is you perceive
Is it something hopeful approaching
or a specter from your past causing you to grieve?

I know you have wounds from another
and between us
they create a schism running very deep
But I have scars of the past too
and now, losing myself in you
My own mind is drifting off to sleep

Staring out there
lost in space
at whatever it is so far away
a new hope or past lamentation
It's difficult for me to tell
and for you to say

So we spent the afternoon
biding fleeting time
staring off into the distance
tending to the wounds
somewhere within our minds
you out there
and me following with my heart
floating away from the present
ever further
ever faster

...and apart

Easy Does It

Eggs over easy
For the prodigal son
Who never left the nest

Encomium to Something Remotely Akin To Learning

After an argument
she left for good, for my own good
and I only love her more
yet again

Freedom

Freedom to or freedom from
Both sound extraordinarily enticing
But if I had to choose
of only one
I think I'd choose freedom from

For if I chose freedom to
I'd be kind of afraid
of some of the things
I just might like to do
potentially at someone else's expense

And I'm pretty sure
the same might be true
as it also pertains to others

Therefore, I think it best
to limit ourselves
to protect us from the trespasses
of everyone else
so that life is pleasant
and we're all safe from the excesses
of one another

Game Theory vs. God Theory:
Living As Though It Truly Matters

I have two theories
Both may or may not
apply to the world

However,
One tells me that even if I sin
I could still possibly win
if no one catches me

The other is absolute
because God always knows the truth
and if God sees me do wrong
he'll punish me in accordance
with his laws

The former
is the morality
of some scientific views of reality
The latter is the morality of religion

And if I had to choose
between the two
I think I'd choose the latter
because if I didn't,
then sin
wouldn't matter
that much
in the end

And if I live life as a game
I could potentially fail by God
But if I live by God

I'll also excel in the former
So, in order
to be safe and secure
more certain
and more assured
that I do right
in the realm of life
I think it might
just be best
to live in accordance

with God theory

I'm A Strange Pantoum

Never do I feel tuned into the times
While living within hapless confusion
Mental illness keeps me so far behind
Lost in a world of my own delusions

While living within hapless confusion
I twiddle my thumbs like Nero's fiddle
Lost in a world of my own delusions
Unable to solve a puzzling riddle

I twiddle my thumbs like Nero's fiddle
Wishing inside I were normal like most
Unable to solve a puzzling riddle
Of how it was I became diagnosed

Wishing inside I were normal like most
I walk awkwardly by, mumbling nonsense
Of how it was I became diagnosed
Others wishing they knew how to comment

I walk awkwardly by, mumbling nonsense
Biding my time on new medication
Others wishing they knew how to comment
A troubling cause of much frustration

Biding my time on new medication
It keeps me going a little longer
A troubling cause of much frustration
Something right now I can only ponder

It keeps me going a little longer
To take my time and stay a steady pace
Something right now I can only ponder
My life is a journey and not a race

To take my time and stay a steady pace
Mental illness keeps me so far behind
My life is a journey and not a race
Never do I feel tuned into the times

In Gratitude

Being alive
is the greatest joy
of which I can conceive
And if I die tomorrow
I believe
it would have been worth
all the sorrows
all the pleasures
the adventures
the moments of boredom
and confusion of ignorance

And whether there is a heaven
and hell
or nothing at all to follow
It's just as well
For either way
I've lived a good life
in spite
of whatever waits
at the end of time

In Trochaic Tetrameter: With Interludes

Come and join this vain endeavor
Journey through great feats of folly
Say you think me rather clever
Hear this song of melancholy
Like a magic incantation
Casts a spell of mysticism
Join a hopeless lamentation
Serving only pessimism

Years I've suffered with depression
Manic with sundry delusions
Fraught with spurts of indiscretion
Guided by childish confusions
Yearning for things unrealistic
Serendipitous I traveled
Through the mires antagonistic
Everything became unraveled
Loves remaining unrequited
Harmed me deeply; left me weeping
Kindred spirits un-united
Now continuously sleeping

Here I lie so apathetic
Slow declining like I'm dying
Lonely hollowed out ascetic
Seeking something edifying
Body laid out deep in slumber
Wrinkled sheets deformed unmoving
Sheep go by; I count their numbers
Knowing life is not improving
Out the window children playing
Screaming without comprehension
Knowing not of what they're saying

Hardly do I pay attention
Shouts of much ecstatic laughter
Great amusement they are sharing
What disturbance follows after?
Lazy me no longer caring
Neighbors wonder with confusion
Why on earth he's so pathetic
Living forlorn in seclusion
Wish I were more energetic
Somber silence dulls expressions
Laying waste my mind completely
While producing strange obsessions
Come and leave perhaps discreetly
Blunders yesterday I ponder
Lead to doubt and disaffection
Chances that I badly squandered
Could have led to new directions
Tell me how to lose this anguish
Heavy forces keep me crumbled
Troubles causing hope to languish
Without promise I am humbled

Suddenly inside of my head
Something as if an angel said
More welcome sound I have not heard
What follows is her every word

"Do not despair; the end is near
This song of sorrow cannot last
Let this music fill up your ears
And do not dwell upon the past
Reprieve is here; come seize the day
Expect despair to rule no more
Uplifting thoughts chase gloom away
A sense of pride we shall restore

As mighty forces intercede
Prevent collapse from seizing hold
To pick you up as was agreed
A life so weary now paroled."

Alas, if only it were true
However, I confess to you
Words above are merely fiction
There was no such interdiction
If only tales like this were real
Oh how it would be so ideal
But life is so much more complex
At times unfair in some respects
And so I leave this lyric ruse
A fiction made just to amuse
Thank you for reading it my friend
I bid you all farewell. The End.

Just Before Waking

I think about death sometimes
I think about it quite a bit
I wonder if anything at all
will come after it
And will it hurt
and even worse
will I cease to exist?

I suspect that dying
will probably be
something very similar
to the way things were
before I was conceived

But what was it like
before I was born?
I can't recall that far back
so I'm not really sure
But I doubt that it was like
anything more
than dreamless sleep

Yes, I've been to oblivion
I go there every night
just for a short visit
in between dreams
to see what it'll be like

And I suspect someday
I'll return
and not just for a sojourn
but rather for a permanent stay

However,
if I may
have a wish fulfilled
for the best way to die
please let me go
just before waking
so I won't need to say…

"Goodbye"

My Coming of Age

To *come of age* is a difficult thing to define
Perhaps an important rite of passage for most
Or a defining moment of transition
And there are many examples of such milestones
For some, coming of age could be graduation from a school or
learning program
For others, the first cigarette smoked
For others still, it may be getting married, having children
Or just having sex for the first time
But usually it's something more or less to celebrate

My coming of age was the day I was first released from
Dominion Hospital
in Arlington, Virginia
One week after I had shown up in my bosses office clutching a bible
And mumbling incoherently
About things I can't remember very clearly
But something happened in that hospital over the course of a
week
It was like a rite of passage into a world that few have
experienced or even wish to
It was a stark, almost overnight change
When I walked into Dominion Hospital in the summer of 1991
I went in the door as one person but walked out the door another
It was a very strange world at first and took some getting
accustomed to
It was difficult to relate to others or talk about my illness
My mother and father hid it from the rest of the family
I was reluctant to discuss it with employers and new
acquaintances
But sometimes I did anyway
I told my friends and they started treating me a little different

Though, bless their heats, they tried to understand
But they couldn't
It was nothing I could adequately explain to them

My Epitaph

I stuck it out
and earned my wings
though others may beg to disagree

However,
after what I've lived through
and continue to
...within
I am my own hero inside
it matters not what others decide
and that is all that matters to me

My Frustration

In the end
it doesn't seem to matter
whether you're right or wrong
only if you're calm

And if we're all headed off a cliff
then it will be the calm ones
who will say,
"Don't get over excited yet"

And in that way
they'll be the only ones
who are still sane
but all equally dead
just the same

My One and Only

She was the first
and so far the only
girl I've ever had

It didn't end very well
and now I can tell
she's very mad

But I did what I had to do
because that's what my parents
Wanted me to

Since I live in their home
So now I'm single
And often sad

No True Harm

My favorite quote comes from Socrates
Well perhaps more accurately
it might be from Plato
"No true harm can come to a good person"
Or so I've heard

I've mulled it over in my mind
many a time
and I think it must be true
for no matter what misfortunes befall you
(and inevitably they will)
it's better not to deserve
than it is to deserve
and that makes all the difference in the world
at least where suffering is concerned

Past the Point of No Return

Diagnosed at age twenty-four
Hospitalized for nearly a week
for having paranoid delusions
Almost catatonic
Hardly able to speak

I was at work
sitting in my boss' office
mumbling incoherently
clutching a bible
fearing for my life
thinking it was all a conspiracy

So I was rushed off
to a psychiatric ward
where they shot me up with meds
Then I was discharged
To a cheaper facility
because my health insurance
wouldn't cover such a disability
But at least I was stabilized
though fatigued all the time
and lying mostly in bed

That happened in the summer of 1991
I've had periodic relapses since then
delusions of grandeur
apocalyptic visions
with periods of depression
now and again

I had no family history
of anyone being mentally ill

nor substance abuse
of anything
that could have produced
such bizarre
but crushing psychoses

So I don't know For sure
where I got these visions
of conspiracy and persecution
However, in a world such as this
with so much violence and prejudice
I suppose it's not improbable
to form such delusions

I can vaguely recall
what it was like
to feel normal,
to belong
However, twenty-eight years
seems like an eternity ago
and after having many episodes
those days seem hopelessly distant
and irretrievably gone

I'm blessed and thankful to be alive
Still, I've worked and lost many odd jobs
At times felt hopeless and depressed
And being dependent on my folks all my life
it's difficult to feel worthy
of dignity and respect

But, medicine has come a long way
in these many years
And improvements in society continue
As some of the stigma associated

with mental illness has disappeared
it gives me some hope
and something promising
to hold on to

I often feel inadequate, burdensome
and harbor many regrets
I can frequently be dark and pessimistic
However, to be most honest
the future holds a great deal of promise
and after studying philosophy in college
I think it best to acknowledge
that despite whatever gloom and futility
even though the world can be unforgiving
it's still very much worth living
because the only acceptable alternative
is to never have lived
And that
Is no longer
A possibility

Pecking Disorder

Bias is great when it's favorable
but not so great when it isn't
I've experienced some of both
and despite being diagnosed
with bipolar disorder
it's been mostly the former
that I have come across

People have various abilities
and characteristics
and sometimes we're judged
based on the most silly
or insignificant difference
and not given a chance to succeed

And I'm sure we all have dreams

Mine was to be a philosopher
and a great one too
But let's not dwell on childish ambitions
Let's talk about the kind of bias
that inhibits and negates its victims

I haven't experienced much of that
at least not as much as some

However, I participated in it
sometimes deliberately
sometimes unknowingly
and sometimes paradoxically
a combination of both
even thinking it was right

But it wasn't

I fought and clawed
over a few shiny things in life
ignorant and blind
and somehow lost sight
of all the damage I was doing

But now I know
And it's not pretty
And living with bipolar
now seems kind of fitting
allowing me to see what it was like
to be on the receiving end
of all my own pecking, prejudice
and spite

And if it were possible
to turn back the clock
reversing time
It would be my wish
To go back and fix
All the souls I broke

... including mine

Poem Using the Word Climb

Every day I try to climb
the steep and perilous
ladder of success
And every day
I stumble and fall
and dust myself off
with all the rest

Feeling like Sisyphus
rolling his boulder
eternally up hill
in many ways
forging onward
with a determined will

However,
to be most honest
And truthful
perhaps I've lied

Instead of climbing
the ambitious ladder
to success
I never even tried

Popularity

I don't think I'll ever be
a very popular person

Of that I'm fairly certain

I'm way past my prime
and running out of time
and besides
it's been my experience
that few want to donate
to my joy and pride

There are much younger
and more mature girls and guys
out there to reward

That's what popularity is for

Seeking Amnesty

Words escape me
But cannot escape these thoughts
Prison of conscience

She Says I'm Batshit Crazy

Solitude is fine
Until I meet a woman
I wish to be with

Spawning Run

Salmon swim upstream
Otherwise face extinction
Dead float down with ease

Starting with a Haiku: One of Arthur's Mayflies

A man grows older
A fish swims upstream to spawn
Gracefully floats down

We started at high tide
Got past the breakers
Fighting the rip current
we hit the beach
at the crack of dawn

Then it was upstream
past the falls
past the predators
on the banks
and in the rapids

And then I...
I got to the shallows inland
all alone

I thought it was for the greater good
I thought it was for science
for money
for glory
for pride
But it was just another spawning run
and like so many before me
I didn't know it at the time

Talk About Being Schizoaffective

First of all
it wasn't my elective
to be schizoaffective

In some ways I may seem different from others
In other ways not

Like anyone else I have my good days and the bad
and the days in between
But I think I may seem more extreme
than others do

On the good days I'm ecstatic
On the bad days I'm depressed
Sure I'm erratic and more so than the rest
But let's not suppose I'm so different from those
who think they need to treat me disparagingly
just because I'm somehow defective
for being schizoaffective

If only I'd broken an arm
or leg
then others wouldn't be so alarmed
and I wouldn't need to beg
to be understood or just feel normal

And we all want to feel normal

Then there are the delusions
some are grand, some are banal,
some paranoid, auditory, visual, but somehow
I think I still qualify to be a human being

No, it's not everyone out there
Most care and that's a great thing
But the world is often cold and cruel all on its own
whether we humans like it or not

Employers don't like to hire
people who are in mentally
dire straights
Too much drama emotionally
for everyone else

Sometimes I think it would be better
to lock myself away out of sight
or to get rid of me altogether
than to put up a fight

Because I feel too much like a burden on society
But it's hard to go quietly into oblivion
So I stick around for another day
or two
just to see what comes my way
before it's through

I suppose it's not the end of the world
being schizoaffective
But it's no picnic
at least not from my perspective

The Crick

I see before me
the winding gravel road to Grandma's house
Stretching along the foot of a small mountain range
paralleling the border of the two Virginias

The woods behind the house
reaching up the steepening slope of the mountain
meet a magnificent amber morning sky
with clouds drifting effortlessly by

The little crick
trickles along the edge of the woods
The crystal clear waters of the spring
from which it begins
were so clean
that we could drink from it

Thunder claps like a drum
And afternoon spring rains
patter against the windows
A cymbal roll
sounding the start of something grand

Fireflies fill the air
on a lazy summer night
like soft flickering Christmas lights
a spectacular symphony
of nature's beauty
as we light fireworks to celebrate the 4th

Autumn leaves
fall from the trees
so brilliant and flamboyant

on a crisp chilly day
floating in a gentle breeze
like confetti ending a celebration

And when winter arrives
the snow is deep and white
as I diligently shovel a solemn path
leading back to the winding gravel road
The air is cold as ice
and sun so bright
climbing up a cloudless sky
to eventually set
behind the mountain

Grandma is gone now
almost twenty years
and now, looking forward
I too fear passing away

But the mountain and the crick
fireflies and autumn leaves
will all hopefully still be
here for a few more generations
until they too are gone
followed eventually by the Sun and Earth
and finally the whole Universe

The entire world—gone

Forever ...

Everything that began
also has an end
But I dare not complain
Isn't finality that which makes the present
a most precious gift?

The Fleeting Present

Time is fleeting
It is now
And yet somehow
we lose sight
of now
and focus on then
Or we look ahead
and again
lose sight of the present

The past can define us
sometimes
But we can still
do something now
that may redefine us
... tomorrow

Luminous Pantouminous

This computer screen is too luminous
It really shines like a florescent light
This computer screen is so ruinous
It is probably going to wreck my life

It really shines like a florescent light
while I play many ridiculous games
It is probably going to wreck my life
or maybe it will just drive me insane

While I play many ridiculous games
the clock of my life slowly ticks away
or maybe it will just drive me insane
with all the mind-destroying games I play

The clock of my life slowly ticks away
like blood draining from a dying body
With all the mind destroying games I play
I really should find another hobby

Like blood draining from a dying body
this computer screen is so ruinous
I really should find another hobby
This computer screen is too luminous

The Unevolutionary Revolutionary

To be a man
To stand tall
and proud
Those are privileges
that I'm not allowed
For I have not yet reached that stage
I've not yet come of age

To own my own home
To have a wife
instead of being alone
traveling through life
Those are blessings
that I've not yet received
For I have not yet reached that stage
I've not yet come of age

To speak with confidence
and certainty
To assert prominence
instead of weakness
and being easy prey to adversity
Those are traits
I do not have
For I have not yet reached that stage
I've not yet come of age

But I'm happy
and still feel blessed
in spite of these things
nevertheless
And I fear challenge, change,
and hardship
I still don't want to reach that stage
That is why I've not yet come of age

Time Wasted

Another Wednesday has come
Much like the last one before
Lying in bed all day
it won't take long to get through

I look back at my life
and all the wasted time
I could have done more worthwhile things
had I truly wanted to

But these regrets do me no good
Though they roll over and over in my head
Thinking of things I could have done
Had I not lain so much in bed

To Be Forgotten

So many people and things forgotten
People I knew and things I did quite often
People and things I may never see or experience again
Some I enjoyed and some I didn't
So many that I can't recall
or even begin
to count them all

But I do remember some
And ruminate on them...each and every one

Memories don't last forever
They eventually fade
into an indiscernible haze
tucked away
in some dusty and remote corner
of gray matter
slowly decaying within the brain

Or perhaps it would be a bit more coherent
to simply call it the spirit
or soul
or psyche
or whatever it might be
that makes us who we are
and not conscious-less automatons

And I do wonder what happens
when all the memories are gone
for good and forever
Will any part of us carry on
somewhere beyond
the realm of the material?

And if not
then will I too merely be
ultimately
no more than someone
that someone else forgot?

To Catherine

Dearest Catherine,

I would give you the world
if I had the world to give
I want you to be happy
for the rest of your life
I want you to have hope
and joy
to see you smile
to hear you laugh
to never worry
never hurt
To wipe away all the tears
and sorrows
and never let them back into your life

If I could move mountains
with bare hands
or part the sea
through sheer will
I'd forge a path
to make your journey
through this world
an easier one

If only I had the world to give...

Sincerely,

Gary

Unsown Seeds

I know I'm lazy
procrastinate
and accomplish almost nothing
There's something very wrong
in my head

However, being crazy
has taken a toll
and I've always known
that seeds I haven't sown
will come back to haunt me
in the end.

With Gratitude

Thank you for good health
a roof over my head
clothes on my back
food in the fridge
and a bed

Without these important needs fulfilled
I'd be homeless, cold, hungry, and ill
or possibly even dead

Thank you for a computer
a car since I'm a commuter
air conditioning and heat
and loving parents
who are still alive

Without these wants assured
I'd be uncomfortable, unloved, and bored
though I could probably still survive

Thank you for literacy
moments of peace and serenity
the good sense to study philosophy
and the company
of good friends who help

Without advantages like these
I'd be ignorant, poor, and lonely
and unable to take good care of myself

But thank you most of all
for the chance to live

time to volunteer and abundance to give
and I apologize
for all I've taken for granted and bad things I've done

For life may be a gift or a test
I still count the many ways I'm blessed
and wouldn't trade places with anyone

Valentine's Haiku

Resplendent flower
Languid, trepid admirer
Left for another

Wrestling with Despair

It takes energy to write a poem and create a rhyme
It takes energy to wrestle with despair sometimes
Despair is like having no will to move forward
like fits and starts that come and go and bottom out

Life is difficult enough to live without despair
Sometimes I think it's just not fair
living with despair

But then!
I think to myself; if there were no such thing as despair
Then there would be…
well…
no despair.

So maybe there's just no silver lining to despair at all
Who needs it? Go away is what I say!
But despair won't listen.
and so it stays.

Despair is like a tortured poem
that doesn't rhyme very well
It's the sort of thing you just can't sell
Because nobody wants to live in it
or be reminded of what it is to despair
because like I say,
there's no silver lining anyway.
So I sort of wallow in it sometimes
at least until it leaves
then I'm fine

Chapter Three
Dark Thoughts

A Hacku

It is better to
Never have loved at all than
Love unrequited

A Requited Love

Pacific Salmon
Floats downstream after spawning
For truth and justice

Abandoned

Many friends have come and left
Now I'm almost alone
and full of regrets
and when the end comes
I doubt it will be said it was anyone's fault
for I suspect nothing will be said
regarding me
at all

Digging My Own Grave

After many mistakes
producing enormous regrets
branded with *mental illness* at age twenty-five
I've let go of any hope
of ever exceeding in life
At least not in terms
with which the virtuous and well-to-do
will ever identify

And for whatever reason
I continued to dig deeper
in the direction already then headed
toward the profound deficit I had
without care, created
while looking for beauty and vitality
in a world I had spiritually desecrated

However,
having now seen what I have done
and unable to confide in God or anyone
since I have doubled down as it were
on wretchedness and debauchery
I'm presented with a horrible dilemma
of whether or not to consider myself anathema
both of which are entirely unconscionable
to her and therefore to me

Doggerel

Hi
I'm Gary
and I'm bipolar
Sometimes it feels
like my life is over

It's just past midnight
and I'm wide awake
I guess drinking all that caffeine
was a big mistake

Now I sit here wired up
and type on these keys
trying to write a poem
that someone will read

This is my fifth draft
and I'm hoping for a hit
But it's looking quite bad
and sounding like...

So I think perhaps
it might be best
if I give up now
and get some rest

Emotional Flatness

I don't like emotional flatness
so I go lie on my mattress
and dream life away
hoping tomorrow will be a better day

But I know inside things won't change
because when you're emotionally flat
it doesn't matter where you're at
Every day is just the same

Epic Failure

Important things to do
and nothing's getting done
It's getting down to the wire
And becoming very worrisome
But I'm not afraid to fail
I've done it many times before
And I'm sure
there will be
many more
times to come

Estranged

I wish I weren't so distant
from people I love
I wish I could be understood
by those I'm distant from

But it's hard to explain
why I behave as I do
and seem so far removed
from people I care about
like you

I suppose I worry
that truth be told
years of alienation and solitude
have rendered me
sterile and cold

Therefore I have seen fit
to cast myself away
from all the rest
out of regard
and fear
that those I hold dear
would be quite appalled
to discover
the disquieting truth
that I don't really love them

... at all

Fleeting Meaning

We give life meaning
The universe is absurd
Time will destroy all

Following My Blithe

Today I was spraying weeds outside
Ruthlessly killing them wherever they lie
The weeds grow by the droves
among the rows
of bushes and flowers we so carefully plant
I killed them for no other reason
Than because I didn't want them there

I sort of wonder if what I did was wrong
killing all those poor things doing me no real harm
Their green leaves produce vital oxygen that I breathe
But I killed them anyway
in spite of this noble deed

I suppose I produce a little CO2 in return
for them to use
so that they can grow back again
And when they do
maybe next time
I'll let them live

For the Sake of Me

Alone, forsaken, broken, and hurt
a solitary man born outside of the church
All he ever sought to pursue were dreams
Illusions that didn't exist at all it seems
And when the day finally came in which he awoke
only to discover his life was a joke
he gazed upon a barren and sterile land
a place he had made with his own two hands
and was shocked and so surprised to see
that his very own name turned out to be *me*

Accepted by Haikuniverse

Monkeys banging on keyboards
Produce disagreement
God speaks

Hanging on to Dear Life

Hanging on a ledge
to avoid falling to my death
My fingers grow weak
as I turn the other cheek
another blow
but they don't know
as they slowly
kill me

When I'm Hopeless

They say to hope for a better future
in a realistic way
From what I know of *realism*
it's nothing more than how things are today
And if that's true
then it seems that nothing will ever change
So what is there to hope for
if everything will just stay the same?

If Women Are Truth

Humans fight for truth
Elephant seals fight to mate
DNA doesn't care

Inappropriate

I'm a stranger to worldly success
an ugly, filthy, and wretched mess
I do things I'm not supposed to do
things of which many would not approve

And yet these terrible things I've done
really don't seem to hurt anyone
However, I feel awful inside
holding back things I'm trying to hide

I wish I could stand tall and proud
and speak of my deeds nice and loud
But that's just the way things seem to be
when I behave inappropriately

Requiem

To have lived instead of merely existed
Is there even such a thing?

I don't know
But from what I can tell
it's not going very well
for anyone in this godforsaken hell
in which we're living

The climate is changing
Species are dying
They say
that galaxies
will someday
be colliding
As our dreams erode
in a universe so cold
and unforgiving

And it makes me quite mad
when I'm told to be grateful
for what I have
I really wonder what that even means

However, such are the woes
of those God never chose
as we endure
persevere
and cling
to that which we hold more dear
than anything

... our sanity

Saying Goodbye

I'm saying goodbye
to someone who was once
a very special friend

I don't think I'll ever see her again

It makes me terribly sad
to forfeit those times we had
but now I believe
she must think me an enemy
from the way we both acted
the last time I saw her

That was pretty bad

I suppose I let her down
but there was little I could do
when my parents wanted me to
stop seeing her

Now I'm alone and lonely
and think if only
I could have just one more chance
at the romance
we had

Self-Flagellation

Beating myself up
The peaceful fight themselves
When at war

The Fire Inside

Like a dragon to be slayed
I stand in the way
of happiness for acquaintances
and friends
bellowing only
fire and acrimony
guarding outside the doors
of heaven
to which others try to ascend

And when my life is over
it will no doubt be said
What a fearsome monster I was
in the end

However, all I can say
God must have wanted me that way
otherwise she would have let me in

Undomesticated

A lion at heart, I needed to be tamed
but things didn't work out quite that way
So wild and feral, I do what I may
and a prisoner of the frontier I have remained

Unkindred

Time flies
at a furious pace
But this is not a race
just life
in a lonely place
called Earth

EPILOGUE

When the end comes
and inevitably it will
in one way or another
were anyone to survive
it ought to be said of our lives
that we appreciated the time
and loved each other ...
until
we said goodbye

Made in the USA
Columbia, SC
28 October 2024

45012885R00081